I0529223

Quiet Influence,

YOU

Real Presence,

SHOULD

and Coaching

BE A

as a Way of Being

COACH

DAPHNE B. LATIMORE

YOU SHOULD BE A COACH

Quiet Influence, Real Presence, and Coaching as a Way of Being

Copyright © 2025 by Daphne B. Latimore.

All rights reserved. No part of this publication may be reproduced, distributed or transmitted in any form or by any means, including photocopying, recording or other electronic or mechanical means, without the proper written permission of the author or publisher, except in the case of brief quotations embodied in critical reviews and certain other non-commercial uses permitted by copyright law.

Paperback ISBN: 979-8-9995436-2-2

Hardback ISBN: 979-8-9995436-3-9

Published by

The Publishing Pad
www.thepublishingpad.com

What Experts Are Saying

"The book is experiential and authentic, reflecting Daphne's true strengths as a strategic influencer and leader."
—**David Ashton,** Senior HR Consultant & Director, MYHR Consultancy

"More than theory, this book is about impact: a call to lead with presence and purpose. Read it, reflect on it, and live it."
—**Jerome L. Haynesworth,** CLTMC, Managing Director, JLHaynesworth & Associates, LLC

"One thing that stood out in You Should Be a Coach was how applicable the content is. The appendix is another gem, with practical templates and conversation starters to return to."
—**Ruthmarie Swisher,** Leadership & Team Effectiveness Director

"You Should Be a Coach is an insightful guide for aspiring coaches, leaders, and those interested in self-coaching. Each chapter is filled with actionable insights on essential coaching skills and thought partnerships, empowering readers to confidently pursue their passions."
—**Karen O. Drake,** MA, PCC, Wellness & Executive Coach

Table of Contents

INTRODUCTION

Includes the distinction between traditional coaching and thought partnership—defining the unique blend of presence, partnership, and perspective that shapes your work.

PART I
What Happens in the Moment

Chapter 1

How early experiences of being "chosen" reveal leadership identity and natural coaching presence.

Chapter 2

Mastering the art of quiet presence, resisting the urge to solve, and creating space for client discovery.

Chapter 3

How coaching happens from any seat, formal or informal, and why influence isn't limited by credentials.

PART II
Coaching as a Way of Being

Chapter 10
Turning insight into meaningful and sustainable action through intentional reflection.

PART III
From Insight to Influence

Chapter 11
Affirms that impactful coaching can happen organically through everyday interactions—without needing a title, certification, or formal recognition.

Chapter 12
How to cultivate a workplace environment where coaching behaviors are modeled and encouraged at every level, regardless of formal roles.

Chapter 13
The unspoken responsibilities of informal coaching, including ethical considerations, confidentiality, and the importance of knowing your limits.

Chapter 14
The path from informal influence to professional coaching: what credentialed practice entails, and the value of informal coaching.

Chapter 15
A contemporary twist on the Island Test, this chapter explores how your unseen presence—in everyday, un-curated moments like waiting in an airport—reveals the kind of leader people trust to navigate ambiguity, even before a word is spoken.

Epilogue

The Moment After the Breakthrough

THEY ALWAYS SAY IT WITH a laugh. Sometimes a raised eyebrow. Often with a mix of relief and disbelief: "You should be a coach."

The thing is . . . I am one.

But what does that really mean? Am I a traditional coach? Or something else?

The truth is, I'm often both a coach and a thought partner, depending on the moment and what's needed.

Traditional coaching is usually a structured process focused on guiding a client through self-discovery, accountability, and skill-building. It's a confidential, goal-oriented relationship that uses specific frameworks and techniques.

Thought partnership is more fluid and collaborative. It's a dynamic dialogue where two minds come together to wrestle with complex challenges, co-create ideas, and navigate ambiguity.

Thought partners bring their own expertise and perspective—not just questions.

My work blends those roles.

Sometimes I'm holding space for quiet reflection and insight, asking powerful questions that unlock a breakthrough.

Other times, I'm right beside my clients in the thick of complexity, challenging assumptions, sharing perspective, and co-creating strategy.

That blend is where the magic happens—the moments that inspire the remark "You should be a coach." Because what clients really experience in these moments is not just coaching in the traditional sense, but a true partnership that sees and honors their full potential.

This book isn't about becoming a coach. It's about what coaching and thought partnership do in the wild. In the moment. In the mess. In the laughter.

It's about what we uncover when we listen beyond the surface. And the power of showing up with just enough presence, pause, and perspective to make room for real insight.

If you've ever held space for someone else's growth, even informally . . . if you've ever asked the question that made the room go quiet . . . this book is for you.

This is also a book about influence—quiet, catalytic, often unrecognized influence. It's about how people who never set out to be "coaches" end up becoming the ones others rely on for direction, clarity, and courage.

In many ways, this book reflects a shift in how we lead. Coaching today isn't limited to certified professionals in closed-door sessions. It shows up in hallway conversations, cross-functional meetings, one-line emails, and hard pauses in the middle of messy moments.

It's a way of being. A way of noticing. A way of guiding from within.

So yes, you should be a coach. But more importantly, you already are, in ways you may not have named.

Let's name them. Let's honor them. And let's explore how your presence, your voice, and your way of thinking might already be shaping the people and systems around you.

Let's talk about what's really happening when they say: "You should be a coach."

What Happens in the Moment

I've had the privilege of working with Daphne as my thought partner for over fifteen years—through every twist and turn of my professional journey. What stands out most is how she shows up not just as a coach, but as a trusted ally who listens deeply, challenges me thoughtfully, and sees possibilities I might have missed on my own.

In those real-time coaching moments—the breakthroughs that happen quietly but powerfully—Daphne's presence is steady and sure. She creates space for insight to surface, helping people discover clarity even amid uncertainty. That ability to be 'chosen' when it matters most is what leadership and coaching are really about.

Part I explores those moments when coaching reveals its true magic: presence, listening, and the courage to ask the right question at the right time.

—Lynn, Chief Marketing Officer

The Island Test

If you were stranded on a desert
island, who would you want
with you and why?

THE FLUORESCENT LIGHTS BUZZED OVERHEAD as we sat in a circle, arms folded, name tags slightly askew from the day's earlier icebreakers. It was the third day of a weeklong team development retreat—the kind that promises insight, growth, and maybe a little awkward bonding.

When the facilitator tossed out the island question, people chuckled. Someone made a joke about needing a chef. Another picked the person with the loudest laugh. But then the tone shifted. As the responses continued, something became clear: This "Island Test" wasn't just a fun game. It was a window into how we saw each other, and how we wanted to be seen.

My name kept coming up. Again and again.

Not because I was the funniest. Not because I'd make the island feel like a vacation resort. But because I'd help us survive. Because I'd figure it out.

That moment, although casual, stuck with me. It was the first time I realized how others viewed me: calm, resourceful, steady. In their eyes, I wasn't just a teammate—I was the person you'd want beside you when things got real.

At first, I dismissed it with a half-smile. "I guess I'm practical," I said. But it made me reflect. Why did people feel that way? What did they see in me that I hadn't named yet?

The room was filled with peers—smart, accomplished professionals. Some were natural entertainers, others were born motivators. And yet, when it came to the island—the unknown, the test of resourcefulness—I was the one they trusted.

What they said in that moment stayed with me:

- "You stay calm when things go sideways."

- "You don't panic—you plan."

- "You're the one who'd figure out how to get us off that island."

It wasn't just what they said—it was how they said it. With certainty. With relief. As if choosing me was obvious.

Over the years, in boardrooms, coaching sessions, retreats, and reorganizations, the same pattern appeared. People came to me when the stakes were high, when the path was unclear, when the team needed direction more than entertainment.

And so, in a way, the work began long before the title. Coaching—real, grounded coaching—often starts with how you show up in uncertainty. It's built in how others experience you when pressure rises.

Everyone has a version of **the Island Test**—a moment when they were chosen not because of their résumé, but because of their presence under pressure. Maybe it was a project gone sideways, a team conflict no one else wanted to touch, or a crisis moment when someone said, "Can you handle this?"

Those are clues. Coaching isn't always something you choose—sometimes, it chooses you.

The Fun vs. Function Dilemma

There was a time when I wondered if I should be more light-hearted, more outwardly charismatic. After all, isn't leadership supposed to inspire excitement?

But I've learned that influence doesn't always look like fireworks. Sometimes it looks like a steady hand on the tiller. It's the kind of presence that whispers "We'll figure this out" when everything feels uncertain. That's the coaching presence—the one that doesn't compete with noise but creates calm.

In coaching, I've come to see that trust is rarely built in the big, performative moments. It's earned in the quiet, steady ones— when someone realizes they're not alone on the proverbial island.

The Coaching Mirror

The Island Test became a mirror. It reflected who I already was, even before I had language for it. Today, when clients invite me into pivotal conversations, they're not looking for entertainment. They're looking for clarity, stability, perspective—the same qualities that led people to pick me in that room years ago.

The truth is, many of us are chosen long before we claim the label of "coach." The question is whether we recognize the signs.

Activity: Desert Island Self-Check

Ask yourself:

- Who do people turn to when things get uncertain?

- What do they say about you in the tough moments?

- What's the consistent feedback—even in jest—that hints at your true leadership presence?

Reflection Prompt

Think back to a moment when someone relied on you in a high-pressure or uncertain situation. What qualities did you bring to that moment? What might that reveal about your coaching or leadership style?

Coaching Style Metaphors

The three coaching styles I see most frequently are:

- **The Compass**, guiding the group's direction.

- **The Shelter**, providing emotional safety.

- **The Firestarter**, sparking action.

Which style of coach are you? You may be all three, but which one do people count on most?

Desert Island Inventory

Write down three times when people relied on you during pressure or uncertainty.

Then ask yourself:

- What was your first instinct in each situation?

- What qualities did people later thank you for?

- What stayed with you afterward, and why?

Sometimes your personal brand is quietly built in how you respond under pressure.

And sometimes, coaching starts with being the person others would pick—without hesitation—to be on the island with them.

The Island Test shows us how others first see our leadership under pressure. But what happens when we turn that same lens inward and start asking deeper questions of ourselves and others? That's the topic of the next chapter.

CHAPTER 2

Holding Space When You Want to Jump In

*They're not asking for the answer—
they're asking to be heard.*

ONE OF THE HARDEST LESSONS for a natural problem-solver is learning not to solve.

Coaching taught me to hold space instead of filling it. To ask rather than advise. To let silence be a strategy.

This plays out most when clients are navigating tough conversations, especially around performance issues or emotionally charged decisions. I've sat across from leaders ready to issue ultimatums or resign on the spot, only to watch their entire posture shift after one question:

"What are you hoping will change if you say that?"

They pause.

They breathe.

And then they begin to hear themselves—not just react to the moment.

Holding space doesn't mean you're withholding support. It means you trust the other person's ability to find their own clarity. It means you can sit with their discomfort without rushing to fix it.

Real Story: From Frustration to Clarity

A mid-level leader I coached was struggling to manage an underperforming employee. She opened the session with:

"What would you do if you were me?"

I could've jumped in with a checklist or directive. Instead, I asked:

"What have you already tried?"

That pause invited reflection. She realized she had never clearly communicated her expectations. Her breakthrough didn't come from my advice—it came from her self-awareness.

Activity: The Pause Prompt

Before you offer someone a solution, ask yourself:

- Have they fully named the problem?

- What have they already tried?

- Can I create more space by asking: "What are you hoping will happen next?"

Coaching Application: Replacing Instinct with Intention

Sometimes we rob people of their own discovery because we're too eager to demonstrate our value. But when we hold back just a little, something powerful happens. Insight arrives. Ownership forms. Breakthroughs stick. Here are some simple shifts that can maximize your impact as a coach:

When your instinct is to:	Try this instead:
Give advice immediately	Ask what they've already considered
Solve the problem	Create space for discovery
Share your experience	Let silence speak, or ask another question

You've seen what coaching looks like in the moment and how it becomes a way of being. Let's widen the lens and explore what happens when that way of being starts to influence systems, teams, and even industries.

CHAPTER 3

You Don't Have to Wear the Title

You're coaching even when
you don't mean to be.

THE MOST POWERFUL COACHING DOESN'T always come from someone with the word *coach* in their title. It comes from the people others trust. The people who listen without judgment. The people who ask the right question at the right time—not to show off, but to show they care.

Over and over again, I've watched people hesitate to own the power of their voice because they don't feel "qualified." But their presence, empathy, and clarity say otherwise.

You don't need permission to influence.

You don't need a certificate to be credible.

You need presence, consistency, and the courage to engage with what matters.

So if you find yourself always being pulled into conversations others avoid . . .

If you're the one they call when things are murky . . .

You're already coaching.

Maybe you're not doing it on purpose, but you are doing it with purpose.

Real Story: The Quiet Coach— Influence Without Intention

A client once shared that every time she left a meeting, people stayed behind just to ask her what she thought. She didn't see herself as a coach. She just saw herself as someone who paid attention and told the truth.

But what she was doing—pausing, asking, reflecting— was pure coaching.

Once she saw that, she began to show up more intentionally.

Not louder. Just more grounded.

Activity: Spot Your Informal Coaching Habits

You might be coaching if:

- People say, "You always help me think things through."

- Others confide in you, even when you're not the boss.

- When asked for advice, you often find yourself responding with questions.

- You're often invited into sensitive or strategic conversations, even outside your official role.

Presence is powerful, but it doesn't require a title. In fact, some of the most meaningful coaching happens without any formal label. Next, let's look at what it looks like to coach from wherever you sit.

CHAPTER 4

What Breakthroughs Really Sound Like

"Wait . . . I've never thought
about it that way."

WE OFTEN IMAGINE BREAKTHROUGHS AS bold
declarations—confident, loud, cinematic. But the truth? Real
insight whispers before it shouts.

Breakthroughs often sound like:

"That's . . . not what I expected to say."

"Wow. I've never looked at it that way."

"That question is going to stay with me."

They come in the form of hesitation, vulnerability, or surprise—
not volume.

They don't announce themselves. They ask to be noticed. In coaching, we're not forcing change. We're making space for people to find it themselves. Often the most powerful thing we can do is pause—and say nothing—when insight is emerging.

Real Story: Coaching the Unspoken Need

During a session, a client was wrestling with whether to leave her role. She kept saying, "I just don't feel seen here."

Instead of asking her about her boss or the team, I simply asked: "What does being seen mean to you?"

She was quiet.

Then she said: "It means not having to prove I belong."

That was her breakthrough. Not the decision, but the truth behind the question.

Activity: Recognize the Language of Breakthrough

Listen for these signs of insight:

- "That's a good question . . ."

- "Hmm . . . I need to think about that."

- "Actually, I've never said this out loud before . . ."

When you hear them:

Pause. Don't rush.

That moment is the work.

Sometimes, the most important breakthroughs are the ones we almost miss. In the next chapter, we turn to the quiet shifts—the moments of insight that change everything without making a sound.

CHAPTER 5

Presence, Humility, Humor, and the Coaching Moment

"You should be a coach."
(said with a laugh, in the moment
after a breakthrough)

IT'S NOT A COMPLIMENT. IT'S a revelation.

When people tell me I should be a coach, they usually laugh. They're joking—kind of. But what they're really saying is: "This moment mattered."

Coaching isn't always formal. It doesn't require deep breathing and a three-point agenda. Sometimes it's just two people being honest in real time.

The key ingredients? Presence, humility, and humor.

Presence

Presence is more than just being in the room. It's being with someone in the moment, fully attuned and undistracted. In coaching, presence means setting aside the urge to fix or impress and instead creating a space where the other person feels truly seen and heard. It's the quiet confidence that says, "I'm here with you—not ahead of you, not behind you, but beside you." Often, it's presence, not answers, that leads to the real breakthrough. That kind of presence doesn't happen by accident—it starts with awareness. That's why, before coaching others, we coach ourselves.

Activity: Coaching Energy Self-Check

Before giving advice, pause and ask:

- Am I grounded and present?

- Am I attached to a specific outcome?

- Is this a moment not for giving advice, but for questioning or holding space?

Coaching is not a performance. It's a posture.

Over time, I developed my own way of understanding presence—what I call **the Presence Lens**. It's how I prepare, relate, and reflect as a coach or thought partner.

My Presence Lens: The Four Ps

- **Perspective.** Can I see the broader system, not just the moment?

- **Permission.** Am I invited in, and am I honoring the person's agency?

- **Pause.** Am I willing to slow down long enough to hear what's not being said?

- **Possibility.** Am I pointing toward what's possible, not just what's wrong?

This lens keeps me grounded when I'm in high-stakes conversations. It also helps my clients shift from reactive to reflective—from "What now?" to "What matters?"

Activity: Presence Self-Check

Before your next conversation, ask:

- What energy am I bringing in?

- What might this person need most—safety, challenge, clarity?

- Am I here to fix, perform, or witness?

Presence is not passive. It's active stillness.

The Presence Lens is how we bring our whole self to a moment—without needing to take it over.

Humility

Humility in coaching is about resisting the urge to be the hero. It means showing up without needing to be the smartest person in the room, and creating space for others to discover their own insight. True humility allows us to hold back our expertise long enough for someone else's wisdom to emerge. It's not about having less confidence, it's about having less ego. It's knowing the power of saying, "I don't have the answer, but I trust you'll find it."

Real Story: The Accountability Mirror

I once worked with a senior leader who was visibly frustrated. "My team just isn't stepping up," she said. "I feel like I'm carrying everything."

I paused, then asked, "How often do you let them fail without stepping in?"

She rolled her eyes. Then laughed.

"Wow. That hit," she said. "Probably never."

In that moment, she realized that her frustration wasn't just about their performance, it was about her presence.

Her need to control. Her discomfort with watching others struggle.

Her breakthrough wasn't about fixing the team. It was about owning her role in the dynamic.

That's humility: being willing to look in the accountability mirror—and laugh, learn, and lead from it.

Humor

"This might sound silly, but . . ."

More often than you'd expect, that's how breakthroughs start.

Coaching often gets branded as heavy. Serious. A space for deep dives and deeper silence. And yes, sometimes it is. But let me tell you—some of the most profound shifts I've witnessed came after the room cracked up.

We weren't laughing *at* people. We're laughing *with* them—at the absurdity of a pattern they've just seen clearly for the first time, at the way we all get stuck in our own heads, at the sheer humanness of trying to grow while juggling a career, a team, a family, and an inbox of 900 unread emails.

In one coaching session, a client said, "I keep having this conversation in my head, and she's not even in the room. I'm arguing with a ghost!" We both burst out laughing. That moment of levity gave us permission to name the tension, and then release it.

Why does humor work in coaching?

- **It disrupts loops.** When someone's stuck, laughter breaks the pattern.

- **It builds safety.** Shared laughter signals trust and emotional availability.

- **It invites truth.** People open up when they're relaxed, not when they're guarded.

I'm not a comedian. I'm not there to entertain. But I do know that the coaching room is one of the few places people get to drop the performance, and sometimes what comes through is funny, freeing, or just real.

Activity: When Humor Is a Signal

Ask yourself:

- Did the client just say something that made us both laugh, but also landed?

- Is humor showing up as deflection, or insight?

- Can we sit in the joy of the moment before we dissect it?

More than once, a client has said, "I had a 'Daphne moment' today—I heard your voice in my head."

Usually, it's followed by a laugh . . . and then, a better decision.

Humor doesn't mean we aren't serious about the work. It means we're human enough to laugh while we do it.

And that, too, is presence.

Now that we've explored how coaching shows up in real moments, let's go deeper. In Part II, we'll look at coaching not just as a practice, but as a way of being.

Coaching as a Way of Being

In my work as a Chief Diversity Officer, having a thought partner who understands the full complexity of leadership and identity is invaluable. Daphne's approach goes beyond formal coaching sessions; it is a way of showing up—holding space for the messy, real parts of being human and leading.

Coaching is not just a set of tools or techniques. It's a mindset and a lifestyle. It's about integrating energy, well-being, and presence into every moment, even when it gets uncomfortable. Part II invites you to explore coaching as a way of being—embracing polarity, whole-person care, and authentic presence.

—Michelle, Chief Diversity Officer

CHAPTER 6

Beyond the Question: Coaching as Thought Partnership and Leadership

There's a point in the conversation
when it stops being coaching and
becomes co-thinking—a shared
journey toward clarity.

MOST PEOPLE SEE COACHING AS the pinnacle—a
high-trust, high-impact practice that helps individuals gain clarity
and move forward. And they're right.

But what happens when your coaching begins to echo beyond
the room? When your language, metaphors, and insights start to
ripple through teams, departments, or even industries?

That's when you've stepped into thought leadership. And it starts with co-thinking—the moment when coaching evolves from questioning to partnering.

Traditional coaching is often framed as a one-way process: the coach asks, the client answers. But the most transformative moments happen when both minds are fully engaged—when it becomes a space of mutual discovery, challenge, and creation.

That's the heart of **thought partnership**.

Thought partnership means:

- Wrestling with complexity together

- Bringing your own perspective, not just asking questions

- Creating new ideas through collaboration

In these moments, you're not just guiding—you're joining. You step into the messiness with your client. You share your thinking, not to advise, but to build with them. You become not just a coach, but a co-creator of insight.

This doesn't diminish the power of questions. Instead, it expands their purpose. Questions become springboards into shared exploration. Silence becomes a space for reflection—for both of you. Ideas begin to bounce, collide, and evolve in real time.

Real Story: Thought Partnership in Action

During a strategic planning session, a client found herself paralyzed by competing priorities. Each option was valid. Each demanded resources. The weight of choosing felt heavy.

I could've defaulted to traditional coaching—asked reflective questions, nudged her back to her values, let her talk her way through it. But what she needed wasn't space to process alone—she needed a partner in the mess.

So I stepped in as a thought partner.

We stood at the whiteboard together, side by side, and built a decision matrix. Not something I handed her—something we created in real time. We mapped trade-offs, explored long-term impact, and aligned on what mattered most.

By the end of the session, she wasn't just clear, she was engaged. Confident. Energized.

And so was I.

That moment reminded me: Some of the most powerful coaching doesn't look like coaching at all. It looks like two people thinking together.

The Difference Between a Coach and a Thought Leader

Coaches help individuals unlock insight, while thought leaders help organizations unlock possibilities. One works in the intimate space of questions and reflection; the other works in the expansive space of models, messaging, and influence.

Here's what that looks like:

Coach	Thought Leader
One-to-one clarity and empowerment	Systemic influence and directional insight
Facilitates client-led reflection	Frames new ideas and conversations
Presence-driven, supportive	Voice-driven, catalytic
Operates privately	Influences publicly (writing, speaking, modeling)

Coaching as the Root of Thought Leadership

The best thought leaders often started out as great coaches. That's because coaching strengthens the core muscles of thought leadership:

- **Deep listening** leads to **powerful observation**.

- **Insightful questioning** leads to **unique framing**.

- **Pattern recognition** leads to **model building**.

Your coaching conversations become a laboratory of human behavior. Over time, you begin to notice recurring themes, metaphors that land, frameworks that resonate. And eventually, you realize: these ideas are worth sharing.

My Journey from Coach to Thought Leader

For years, I didn't call myself a coach, and certainly not a thought leader. I simply showed up, listened, asked good questions, and helped people get unstuck. But as time went on, something shifted.

Clients started quoting me. Teams adopted my language. Ideas I had shared in one conversation showed up in other rooms. That's when I realized: I wasn't just coaching anymore. I was shaping thinking.

Frameworks like the Island Test (chapter 1), the Presence Lens (chapter 5), and Polarity Maps (chapter 8) weren't just helping individuals; they were becoming tools for organizations. I had become a thought partner—not just with people, but with systems.

Activity: Are You Becoming a Thought Leader?

- Do others cite or quote your insights outside the coaching room?

- Have your frameworks been adopted in wider settings?

- Are you writing, teaching, or speaking with increasing frequency?

- Do your ideas help others shift how they think—not just what they do?

Thought leadership doesn't require a platform, but it creates one.

It doesn't require a title, but it earns one.

You don't have to stop being a coach to start being a thought leader. You simply have to recognize when your insights begin to scale.

You start as the person on the island . . .

You become the one who maps the island.

Then you help others reimagine what's possible beyond it.

Thinking together is powerful, but coaching the whole person means going beyond thinking. It means attending to energy, emotion, and identity. Next, let's dive into what that looks like.

CHAPTER 7

Coaching the Whole Person

People don't bring just their roles—
they bring their lives.

THE IDEA OF COACHING THE whole person isn't new, but in practice, it's often underdeveloped. Too many conversations focus solely on performance metrics, task lists, or outcomes. While those matter, coaching becomes transformative when it acknowledges the full range of what a person brings into a room—their energy, identity, mindset, fears, rhythms, beliefs, and aspirations.

Coaching the whole person means seeing beyond the role, beyond the résumé, and even beyond the behavior. It means asking, "What's really going on here?"—not just about the work, but in the person's life, their well-being, their self-narrative.

I've coached high performers who looked like they had it all together—hitting goals, leading teams, getting promoted. But underneath that was exhaustion, a disconnection from purpose, or a voice in their head whispering, "This isn't sustainable." Coaching the whole person gives that voice space to speak.

This doesn't mean becoming someone's therapist or overstepping boundaries. It means honoring that people are not machines— they are layered, dynamic, and human. And when you coach the human, the performance tends to follow.

Energy, Identity, and Role

Start by noticing which "self" someone is speaking from. Are they answering from:

- Their role? ("As the VP, I have to . . .")

- Their training? ("I've always been told . . .")

- Their fear? ("If I don't, then . . .")

- Their authentic voice? ("What I really want is . . .")

When we don't acknowledge the whole person, we often coach only the mask—the part that's socially acceptable, promotable, or polished. Coaching the whole person means we help them reconnect to their values, their rhythms, and their sense of meaning.

This is where wellness intersects with leadership. It's why I encourage clients to develop wake-up and wind-down routines—not for productivity, but for presence. Because the way you enter your day and the way you close it has everything to do with how you lead in between.

Real Story: When Rest Was the Breakthrough

A senior leader came to a session drained. On paper, she was managing everything: new initiatives, team transitions, board expectations. But her energy was gone. Not in a burned-out way—in a hollowed-out way.

I didn't ask her to strategize. I asked her to stop talking. We sat in silence.

And then I asked, "What do you think your body is trying to tell you?"

That cracked something open. She realized she hadn't truly rested—emotionally, mentally, spiritually—in months. We spent the session not building plans but creating space. She later told me it was the most productive conversation she'd had all quarter.

She recognized that the breakthrough was not in doing more, but in giving herself permission to pause.

This is coaching the whole person.

Activity: Whole-Person Coaching Prompts

Use these questions to go deeper in conversation:

- What's the story you're telling yourself about this?

- What part of you is speaking right now—your role or your values?

- What would it look like to honor your energy instead of overriding it?

- When do you feel most like yourself?

Integration Over Balance

People often ask me, "How can I balance it all?"

But coaching the whole person isn't about balance; it's about integration. It's asking how work, family, rest, identity, and ambition live together in the same person. Because there is no such thing as work–life balance when your nervous system doesn't know the difference between a deadline and a distress signal. The body keeps score. The heart does, too.

So we coach the whole person—not to fix them, but to remind them they are already whole, and the coaching is simply to help them come back to themselves.

When we coach the whole person, we don't just help them perform—we help them return to who they are. Coaching the whole person means recognizing that stress, energy, identity, and environment shape how someone shows up.

Daily routines aren't fluff—they're anchors for leadership presence. Encouraging wake-up and wind-down rituals helps clients build resilience and clarity.

The Integrated Professional

I often use the term **integrated professional** to describe the client we're coaching toward—someone who doesn't compartmentalize their ambition, leadership, health, or humanity, but instead aligns them.

The integrated professional isn't trying to be perfect in every role.

They're asking better questions:

"What do I need today to show up well?"

"What's sustainable, not just successful?"

"Where can I lead from wholeness instead of exhaustion?"

As coaches, our job isn't to pull people apart into neat categories. It's to help them stitch together a style of life and leadership that feels authentic, grounded, and adaptable.

When the professional is integrated, decisions become clearer. Presence becomes stronger. And leadership becomes sustainable.

That's what it means to coach the whole person.

Activity: Wake-Up and Wind-Down Prompts

Wake-up prompts:

- **What energy do I want to bring?** Take three deep breaths and summon that energy forth.

- **What do I need today?** Identify your intentions for the day.

- **What is my non-negotiable today?** Prioritize your intentions.

Wind-down prompts:

- **What can I release from today?** Identify the day's triggers of concern. If it doesn't warrant further concern, let it go.

- **What am I grateful for?** Reflect on one success from your day.

- **How will I reset?** Visualize rest and recovery.

Helping people navigate themselves is one thing. Helping them navigate opposing tensions is another. That's where polarity thinking becomes essential. We'll talk about polarity thinking in the next chapter.

CHAPTER 8

Practicing Polarity Thinking in Real Life

When both answers are true,
what do you do?

THE MOMENT I MENTION POLARITY management—a concept articulated by Polarity Management's Barry Johnson, PhD—I usually get a loud sigh.

That's not because the concept is hard, but because it asks something deeper of the leader in front of me. It's not about fixing a problem. It's about managing a tension that won't go away.

I ask: "Is this a problem to solve... or a situation to manage?"

That's the turning point.

One of the most liberating shifts in my coaching practice came when I stopped trying to resolve every tension and instead started helping clients navigate polarities—the natural, ongoing tensions that don't have a single "right" answer.

Work/life. Innovation/stability. Structure/flexibility. Being/doing. These are not problems to solve. They are polarities to manage.

In leadership, polarity thinking helps us move beyond either/or thinking and develop what I call the "and" muscle—the ability to hold space for two truths at once. Most of the resistance I encounter in my work with teams comes not from a lack of ideas, but from a belief that only one way can be right.

Real Story: Empowerment AND Accountability

In a coaching engagement with a senior leader, we explored why her team kept stalling. She wanted people to take ownership, but she also wanted quality results.

What we uncovered was a polarity:

- Empowerment without accountability feels aimless.

- Accountability without empowerment feels controlling.

The solution wasn't to choose one—it was to intentionally toggle between both, based on context. That shift transformed how she led her weekly meetings.

Activity: Spot the Polarity

Ask yourself:

- Are both sides valuable?

- Is the tension ongoing or recurring?

- Does favoring one side too long create problems?

If yes, you're in a polarity.

Then explore:

- What's the upside of each side?

- What's the risk of over-favoring either?

- What early warning signs show you're leaning too far?

This is leadership maturity—holding complexity without collapsing into extremes.

Polarity thinking isn't about balance. It's about rhythm. In practice, that means recognizing when two priorities matter equally, holding steady in one while leveling up in the other. The next chapter, Paint the Wall, is about creating that pause—the moment you shift from reacting to responding, so you can protect what's working while advancing what needs to grow.

CHAPTER 9

Paint-the-Wall Moments: Coaching in the Pause

Sometimes the most powerful **move**
isn't action — it's the **pause** that
keeps you from making the wrong
one. In my coaching practice, there's a
term my clients know well:
the Paint-the-Wall Moment.

IT'S THAT SPLIT SECOND WHERE something inside says, "Do it."

Hit Send. Say the thing. Slam the door. Take the action that feels righteous, justified—maybe even overdue.

And yet . . . something else whispers: "Wait."

That moment—that pause—is the fork in the road between reaction and response.

The name came from a conversation with a senior leader who called me after a particularly intense meeting. "I think I just painted the wall," she said.

She wasn't talking about literal paint. She meant that she had let her frustration spill out in a way that colored the entire room—with tone, energy, and tension.

The team was quiet. The damage was done.

"Once the paint is on the wall," she said, "you can't un-see it."

And just like that, a new coaching metaphor was born.

The Anatomy of a Paint-the-Wall Moment

A paint-the-wall moment usually begins with a trigger—perhaps a snide comment, a missed deadline, or a breaking point after holding it together for too long.

But it's not the situation that defines the moment.

It's the urgency to act without awareness.

Clients describe it as a surge—heat in the chest, a quickened pulse, tunnel vision. It feels like clarity, but it's actually adrenaline. It feels like justice, but it might just be ego.

Left unchecked, that surge becomes action.

And the action becomes aftermath.

What Makes This a Coaching Moment?

"Paint the wall" isn't just a catchy metaphor—it's the basis for a coaching tool grounded in emotional intelligence, self-regulation, and presence.

It teaches clients to:

- Recognize their own internal signs of escalation

- Build muscle memory around pausing

- Make decisions rooted in intention, not impulse

- Rewrite patterns of reactivity with practices of reflection

In a world that rewards speed, this tool rewards pause.

Activity: Are You About to Paint the Wall?

Teach people to ask themselves:

- Am I reacting to this moment, or to a build-up of previous moments?

- Would I be okay if this email/text/statement were read aloud in front of a room?

- If I wait fifteen minutes, will I still feel the same urgency?

Sometimes the best coaching tool is silence. Sometimes it's a pause. And sometimes it's teaching someone to recognize their own paint-the-wall moment before it happens.

Why "Painting the Wall" Sticks

Clients love this metaphor because it's vivid, human, and a little bit humorous. We've all painted the wall at some point, whether at home, in a meeting, or in traffic. But giving that moment a name changes the story.

It shifts it from shame to skill.

From reaction to reflection.

From regret to reset.

And that's what coaching is all about.

The Coaching Invitation: Pause, Don't Paint

I teach my clients that when they feel a paint-the-wall moment approaching, they have a tool they can use:

Pause, don't paint.

Sometimes that pause looks like taking three deep breaths.

Sometimes it's drafting the email but not sending it.

Often, it's texting me—"I'm having a paint-the-wall moment"— and letting the act of reaching out interrupt the reaction.

And more often than not, by the time they've paused long enough to name the moment . . . they no longer need to act on it.

That's the brilliance of this tool: it's not about suppression.

It's about awareness.

And in that awareness, choice returns.

Coaching in the Wild

We often think of coaching as something that happens in formal sessions. But real life doesn't schedule itself around your calendar. People have breakthroughs at 2:00 AM. Or on a Tuesday in traffic. Or three minutes before a board meeting.

When clients "hear Daphne" in their heads, it's not about me being right—it's about them having internalized the pause.

They've learned to:

- Slow down before pressing Send
- Ask, "What's really going on here?"
- Choose to respond rather than react

That's coaching.

Not everything needs a reaction. But everything deserves reflection.

The best coaches aren't just heard in the room. They're heard in the moments when no one else is around.

Sometimes the most powerful move isn't action — it's the pause that keeps you from making the wrong one.

A Paint-the-Wall moment isn't just about stopping yourself — it's about being present enough to notice what the pause is revealing. That's the opening for something deeper: turning that awareness into intentional action.

And that's where the real work begins.

Because the pause is only the doorway. What you do next—how you unpack it, make meaning from it, and decide your next move—is what transforms a moment of restraint into lasting change.

That's the work of the debrief.

CHAPTER 10

The Debrief Is the Work

Insight is powerful, but meaning is
where change begins.

THE MOMENT OF INSIGHT IS not the finish line. It's the doorway. The real work happens when we ask: Now that I see this, what does it mean? And what will I do with it?

In coaching, that moment is called **the debrief.**

It's where we slow down, make meaning, and begin the transformation process—not just by thinking, but by integrating insight into lived experience.

We often assume that insight alone will lead to action. But without pause, reflection, and integration, most insights fade into the background. The debrief helps keep them alive.

Whether it's after a behavioral assessment, a breakthrough session, or even a team experience, the debrief is the moment insight takes shape—transforming from a powerful idea into a deliberate, actionable strategy.

Why the Debrief Matters

When clients leave a coaching session without debriefing:

- They may feel "inspired" but unclear on next steps.

- They may forget what actually shifted.

- They lose the opportunity to commit—to themselves or others.

But when we hold space for debrief:

- Clients internalize the learning.

- They name what matters most.

- They begin to build accountability.

Debriefing is not just a reflection technique—it's a presence practice.

It reminds us that coaching isn't about how fast we move ... but how deeply we integrate what we now know.

And let's be honest: insight without a debrief is like buying workout clothes and thinking you're in shape. It feels productive in the moment, but the change sticks only when you do the work.

So we debrief. We pause. We ask the question behind the question. Because the magic isn't just in what they realized. It's in what they do next.

Activity: Post-Insight Debrief

Try asking:

- What stood out most to you?

- What surprised you?

- What will you do differently tomorrow?

- What will you pay closer attention to?

- How will you know it's working?

These questions turn reflection into intention, and intention into behavior.

A Personal Practice

I often close coaching sessions with one final prompt:

"What's the one sentence you're walking away with?"

This distillation moment does more than summarize. It anchors. It moves the experience from abstract to embodied.

That sentence becomes the bridge between the coaching room and the real world.

Coaching doesn't end when the client nods. It begins when they translate insight into movement.

The debrief is the work.

From Insight to Influence

When I took on the challenge of transforming a local newspaper publishing company, I quickly realized I needed more than strategy—I needed a thought partner. Daphne's presence and perspective helped me navigate complexity and ambiguity with confidence.

Coaching often evolves into something bigger: a partnership that influences culture, leadership, and teams beyond individual conversations. It's about moving from insight to real influence—becoming the coach others didn't even know they needed.

Part III invites you to step fully into that broader impact.

—**Scott, CEO**

CHAPTER 11

The Power of Coaching Without the Label

*You don't have to call it
coaching for it to matter.*

THERE'S A QUIET KIND OF power in being the person others turn to—not because of your title, but because of how they feel after talking to you.

You may not carry the word *coach* in your job description. You may never say, "I'm coaching you right now." And yet, the work is happening. The insight is forming. The breakthrough is unfolding.

You are already doing the work of coaching—you're just doing it without the spotlight.

This kind of coaching doesn't require credentials. It requires presence. It doesn't start with a formal intake form—it starts with a question, a pause, or a moment of genuine curiosity. It's woven into hallway conversations, staff meetings, difficult one-on-ones, or impromptu debriefs over coffee.

You listen. You reflect. You hold space. And most importantly—you don't rush in to fix. You create room for someone else to see themselves more clearly.

That is coaching. And it's powerful.

Influence Without Announcement

One of the reasons people hesitate to call what they do "coaching" is because they assume coaching must look a certain way—scheduled, scripted, or certified. But at its core, coaching is a posture, not a platform. It's a commitment to both presence and partnership.

And here's the important distinction:

Informal coaching doesn't replace professional coaching. It reflects the reality that the coaching mindset can—and should—show up in everyday leadership.

When you show up in service of someone else's clarity—without an agenda—you are coaching.

When you do this repeatedly, intentionally, and with integrity, you build a kind of influence that doesn't need to announce itself. People just know you're someone who helps them think, feel, or lead more clearly.

That's what people mean when they say, "You should be a coach."

They're not saying you need to hang a shingle.

They're naming the role you already play—the one that helps others find their next step.

Professional coaches do this with skill, ethics, and structure. But the coaching spirit—the essence of presence and partnership—belongs to all of us.

Activity: Quiet Coaching Self-Check

Reflect:

- Who do people come to again and again?

- What's different for them after a conversation with you?

- How do you create safety, not just strategy?

- Can you trust your influence without a nameplate?

You don't need a title to have impact.

You don't need a credential to coach with clarity.

You just need to recognize the value of the space you hold—and honor it.

You don't have to call it coaching for it to change someone's life. You just have to show up and care—with intention, presence, and trust.

CHAPTER 12

Building a Coaching Culture

It's not just about what you do—
it's about who you empower.

IF COACHING IS A WAY of being, then building a coaching culture is about embedding that way of being into the very fabric of your team or organization.

Not everyone will be a professional coach. Not everyone needs to be. But in a coaching culture, everyone is expected to lead with curiosity, hold space for learning, and engage in meaningful dialogue.

That's why the phrase *"You should be a coach"* isn't just a compliment—it's a call to action. It's an invitation to bring the mindset, practices, and presence of coaching into your leadership, your influence, and your culture.

What Is a Coaching Culture?

A **coaching culture** exists when coaching behaviors are part of how people interact, manage, and lead, regardless of role or title. It shows up in how feedback is given, how decisions are made, and how people grow.

In a coaching culture:

- Questions are valued as much as answers.

- Conversations prioritize development, not just direction.

- Feedback is continuous and two-way.

- Managers coach, not just direct.

- Team members are empowered to think, reflect, and act with ownership.

It's not about everyone becoming a coach. It's about making coaching behaviors a shared norm.

You Don't Have to Be the Boss to Build Culture

Culture doesn't shift from the top down. It shifts conversation by conversation.

If you are coaching, even without the title, you are already influencing culture:

- When you choose not to rescue someone, but ask what they need

- When you pause instead of react

- When you give feedback with curiosity, not criticism

You are modeling what's possible. And people notice.

Coaching Behaviors Everyone Can Use

- Ask before you advise. "What have you already tried?" . . . "What do you think would happen if you did nothing?"

- Listen to understand, not to fix. Sometimes, people need space to hear themselves think.

- Challenge assumptions respectfully. "Is that a fact, or something we've always believed?"

- Model reflection. Share your own learning moments, pivots, and insights.

- Hold space in meetings. Allow room for questions, not just updates.

Barriers to a Coaching Culture
(and How to Shift Them)

When you hear:	Try this:
"We don't have time."	Insert micro-coaching moments into existing conversations.
"That's HR's job."	Normalize development as everyone's responsibility.
"We don't know how."	Introduce a few powerful questions and build from there.
"People won't open up."	Keep trying. Trust builds when curiosity is consistent.

Culture change doesn't require a revolution. It requires repetition.

Activity: Coaching Culture Mini Audit

Ask your team:

- When was the last time someone asked you a powerful question?

- Do you feel safe disagreeing or challenging ideas?

- When you receive feedback, does it feel like a judgment or a gift?

- How often do we pause to reflect together—not just execute?

- Do we celebrate learning, or just results?

Becoming a Multiplier of Coaches

When people say, "You should be a coach," consider this: what if your greatest legacy isn't being the coach, but inspiring others to coach?

What if your influence helps spark a shift where coaching is no longer an exception but an expectation?

Coaching cultures aren't built by programs alone. They're built by people. People like you.

And when you show up with presence, possibility, and permission, you're already leading the way.

Real Story: Turning Culture into a Coaching Ground—A Division-Level Transformation

In a midsized national organization, one business division was experiencing growing pains. Recent leadership changes, unclear team roles, and siloed communication patterns had created a tense working environment. En gagement had plateaued, and performance conversations felt transactional rather than developmental.

Assessments showed that while technical expertise was strong, people leadership was lagging. Managers were focused on output, but team members weren't growing. The division head recognized that to create long-term change, the company needed to embed coaching behaviors—not launch another compliance-driven training initiative.

Rather than rolling out a formal coaching program, the leadership team began using a guiding principle: "Everyone has the capacity to coach."

Weekly team meetings began with a "pause and reflect" moment, encouraging managers to model curiosity.

Managers received simple tools for coaching-style conversations, like:

- "What support do you need to move forward?"

- "What might you try differently next time?"

- "What does success look like for you—beyond the task?"

A peer reflection circle was piloted, allowing staff to coach each other around current challenges and decisions.

Within six months:

- Engagement scores increased noticeably.

- Managers reported fewer bottlenecks and more peer-led problem-solving.

- Coaching language started showing up organically in meetings, one-on-ones, and even email communications.

- Employees began to say things like "That felt like a coaching moment," or "Thanks for helping me think that through."

By positioning coaching as a shared behavior—not a role or title—the organization normalized feedback, built trust, and developed internal capacity for leadership at all levels. Coaching wasn't just something leaders did; it became part of who the entire company was becoming.

The Ethics and Boundaries of Informal Coaching

Just because they trust you doesn't
mean you should carry it all.

WHEN YOU'RE THE PERSON OTHERS naturally turn
to, it's easy to fall into the rhythm of coaching conversations without pause. You listen. You reflect. You help them move forward.
And most of the time, it's deeply meaningful—for both of you.

But there's a fine line between helping and overstepping.

Whether you hold a formal coaching title or simply embody a
coaching presence, ethical awareness and boundary clarity are
essential. Especially in informal coaching—hallway moments,
peer conversations, or quick chats after meetings—the lines can
blur quickly.

This chapter is your anchor. It's a reminder that good coaching is never boundaryless—it's grounded, intentional, and rooted in mutual respect.

What Are Coaching Boundaries, Really?

Boundaries aren't about building walls. They're about clarity:

- What role are you playing?

- What is, and isn't, your responsibility?

- What's needed from this conversation?

In informal settings, you may be someone's peer, friend, boss, or HR partner. Coaching in those dynamics isn't impossible but it does require a heightened sensitivity to:

- Power dynamics

- Emotional safety

- Confidentiality

- The potential for dual roles

Knowing where your influence ends—and when to step back—is part of your professionalism.

When Coaching Crosses a Line

It might be time to pause or redirect when:

- You feel emotionally responsible for their outcome

- You're holding more urgency than they are

- You're giving advice instead of asking questions

- You're navigating topics better suited for therapy, legal advice, or HR compliance

- You notice the relationship shifting toward dependency

The goal isn't to detach—it's to stay present *within* your scope.

Respecting Confidentiality

When someone shares something vulnerable, it's a gift. But if you're not in a formal coaching relationship, it's even more important to clarify what will be kept private and what can't be.

Say this: "Thank you for trusting me. Just so we're clear, if this crosses into something that impacts the team or workplace safety, I may need to escalate, but I'll be transparent with you if that happens."

Boundaries build trust, not walls.

When to Refer or Redirect

You don't need to have all the answers. In fact, part of ethical coaching is knowing when someone else is better equipped to help. Offer to:

- Recommend a therapist, counselor, or EAP resource

- Connect them with HR or legal if workplace compliance is involved

- Pause the conversation until clarity on roles is established

This is especially important for leaders, people managers, and HR professionals who often coach and guide in tandem with organizational responsibilities.

Redirect by saying: "This sounds like something that deserves more dedicated space. Would you be open to talking with someone who's better positioned to support that?"

The Cost of Unclear Boundaries

When we coach without boundaries, we risk:

- Burnout

- Resentment

- Breached trust

- Role confusion

- Ethical missteps

But with clear grounding, coaching becomes more sustainable—for you and for them.

Activity: Ethical Coaching Check-In

Before you lean in, ask:

- What role am I playing right now?

- Is this conversation within my capacity and scope?

- Am I helping them move forward, or am I trying to carry it for them?

- Would a referral better serve them?

- Am I being honest about my own emotional boundaries?

Ethical, informal coaching is an act of leadership.

It's presence with discernment. Compassion with clarity. Support without saviorhood.

The most powerful coaches don't say yes to everything.

They say yes to what is theirs and empower others to find what's theirs, too.

CHAPTER 14

Coaching as a Profession— Beyond the Moment

"At what point does this become more than just what I do naturally?"

THAT'S THE QUESTION I OFTEN hear from people who've been informally coaching for years. They've led teams. Held space. Asked the right questions. Been the person others turn to for clarity and breakthrough. And eventually, they begin to wonder:

Is this something I should formalize? Certify? Make a profession?

The short answer? Maybe. But it depends on your purpose.

Coaching can live beautifully in the informal—as a way of being, a leadership lens, a presence you bring into every room. But coaching as a profession is something else. It's intentional. Structured. Held to standards. And it comes with responsibilities, ethics, boundaries, and continuing development.

And here's the truth: Both are valid. Both are powerful. But they serve different purposes.

Informal Coaching: Influence in the Moment

Informal coaching is often how it starts. You:

- Ask great questions.

- Hold space in meetings.

- Guide others to clarity without giving all the answers.

You're doing it instinctively. And people respond. They trust you, seek you out, and maybe even say, "You should be a coach."

This kind of coaching is deeply valuable, especially in roles like HR, people leadership, DEI, project management, or culture transformation. It's a powerful competency. But it doesn't require credentialing.

Professional Coaching: Structure with Intention

When you move from "doing coaching" to being a coach, things shift.

Professional coaching:

- Uses defined frameworks (such as ICF Core Competencies, GROW, or Co-Active)

- Is grounded in contracts, confidentiality, and ethics

- Is often credentialed (for example, ACC, PCC, or MCC)

- Includes ongoing supervision, reflection, and training

- Requires the ability to manage boundaries and power dynamics

Professional coaching is a discipline—a craft. And yet, the heartbeat is the same as informal coaching: presence, pause, and powerful listening.

So why go professional? Some do it to:

- Create a formal coaching practice

- Work independently or consultatively

- Add structure to an internal coaching role

- Deepen their effectiveness and credibility

But going professional doesn't mean abandoning who you are. It means sharpening your focus.

Pathways to Becoming a Professional Coach

There is no single road to becoming a professional coach but all credible paths require a commitment to skill, ethics, and continuous learning. The International Coaching Federation (ICF) and other professional bodies set rigorous standards that ensure coaches are grounded in core competencies and ethical guidelines.

Many coaches begin with formal training through accredited programs, pursuing credentials such as the Associate Certified Coach (ACC), Professional Certified Coach (PCC), or Master Certified Coach (MCC). These pathways include structured education, mentorship, observed coaching hours, and assessments that test both knowledge and application.

Others integrate coaching into an existing professional discipline, such as HR, organizational development, consulting, or leadership, while still adhering to professional coaching standards. They complete specialized training, follow ethical guidelines, and embed coaching skills into their daily work.

My own journey reflects this integrated approach. I made a deliberate choice not to pursue a standalone coaching designation, instead leaning into my professional credential as a Senior Professional in Human Resources (SPHR) and extensive leadership training. I've trained through the Center for Executive Coaching, Tilt365's Laser-Focused Coaching program, and Lee Hecht Harrison, and completed executive leadership programs at Oxford University's Saïd Business School and the University of New Hampshire.

Coaching is woven into how I lead, consult, and strategize, enabling me to coach leaders in the context of organizational culture and business outcomes.

Whether you pursue coaching as a dedicated profession or integrate it into your broader role, the essentials remain the same: a foundation in proven methodologies, a commitment to ethical practice, and the humility to keep learning.

Coaching has multiple entry points—both can be equally impactful when practiced with skill, integrity, and intention. The key is choosing the pathway that best aligns with your goals, strengths, and the impact you want to make.

Two Primary Pathways to Coaching

Pathway	Description	Common Credentials & Training	How It's Applied
Full-Time Professional Coach	Coaching is the primary professional identity. The coach works with individuals, teams, or organizations as their main service offering.	ICF credentials (ACC, PCC, MCC), Center for Executive Coaching, Hudson Institute, Co-Active Training Institute, Institute for Coaching Innovation, or college coaching certification.	Works with clients in structured engagements focused on personal or professional growth, leadership development, or performance improvement
Integrated Coaching Professional	Coaching is embedded within another professional role (e.g., HR leader, OD consultant, executive, strategist).	Specialized coaching programs (e.g., Tilt365 Laser-Focused Coaching, Lee Hecht Harrison, Center for Executive Coaching), professional certifications (e.g., SPHR, OD, behavioral assessments).	Uses coaching skills to enhance strategic advising, leadership facilitation, and organizational transformation within the scope of their primary role.

From Coach to Thought Partner

For many, the natural progression from informal coaching is to pursue professional training and credentials. For others, it's expanding their coaching approach into a broader methodology—one that blends the principles of coaching with strategic thinking, organizational insight, and cultural influence.

That was my path. Coaching gave me the tools to hold space for others; strategic facilitation and advisory work taught me how to shape the conversation itself. Over time, my method evolved to pair deep listening with bold questioning, and reflection with action.

This is the work of thought leadership. It's not about having all the answers. It's about helping others ask better questions, and giving language to what they already feel.

As a thought leader:

- I translate emerging patterns into meaningful insights.

- I connect operational realities to human behavior.

- I shape frameworks that help people make sense of change.

- I model what it means to be both reflective and action-oriented.

My background—leadership studies, executive coaching, HR strategy, and years of organizational transformation—allows me to speak across layers: individual, team, and system. That perspective is what I offer—not just advice but a way of seeing.

Thought leadership isn't a departure from coaching—it's an expansion. It's the natural evolution when presence, strategy, and influence intersect, enabling you to help others navigate what is and imagine what could be.

Activity: Is Thought Partnership Your Next Move?

Ask yourself:

- Do others seek you out for how you think, not just what you know?

- Are you often connecting the dots others haven't seen?

- Do you feel called to shape bigger conversations—inside or outside your organization?

- Are you creating language, frameworks, or models that help others lead?

If yes, you may already be operating as a thought leader. Own it. Develop it. And bring it forward with intention.

Coaching isn't just something you do—it's someone you become. It's the way you listen, the questions you ask, and the space you hold. Whether it's woven into your role, your calling, or your profession, it becomes part of how you move through the world.

So when someone says, "You should be a coach," you can smile, knowing you already are.

And from there, the choice is yours: to shape it intentionally, to let it shape you, and to leave a legacy defined not just by what you achieved, but by how you helped others step into their own clarity and power.

CHAPTER 15

The Airport Test

If you were stuck at the airport for
hours, who would you call?

IT'S NOT AS DRAMATIC AS the Island Test—no wild
animals, no survival tactics—just humanity at its most frazzled.
Crying babies. Overpriced snacks. A dead phone battery and
nowhere to sit.

And yet, when I've asked this question—"Who would you call
if you were stuck at the airport?"—in workshops, the answers
are just as revealing.

People say:

- "Someone who could help me reframe the situation."

- "Someone who wouldn't panic when things change
  suddenly."

- "Someone who could help me laugh, think, and maybe
  even figure out a new route."

In short: someone who coaches, even if they don't call it that.

Coaching isn't always about structure, strategy, or certifications. Sometimes it's about presence in the middle of chaos, the calm in the delay, the ability to help someone see not just what's broken but what's possible.

Just like the Island Test, **the Airport Test** reminds us that people don't always choose the loudest or most entertaining person—they choose the one who helps them navigate uncertainty with grace, clarity, and just enough humor to keep going.

So if people keep saying to you, "You should be a coach," it might be because . . .

- You're the one they trust in the messy moments.

- You offer perspective when plans fall apart.

- You listen without fixing.

- You show up, even when the gate keeps changing.

That's what coaching really is.

It's not about having all the answers. It's about helping others find theirs, even in the terminal.

And if you've made it this far in the book, I'm going to go ahead and say it again:

You should be a coach.

Or maybe . . .

You already are.

What They Really Meant Was . . .

WHEN SOMEONE SAYS, "YOU SHOULD be a coach," they may be joking.

They may be in awe.

They may be naming something they can't quite define.

But what they're really saying is:

- "You made me feel seen—without needing to be the expert."

- "You created clarity in a moment that felt chaotic."

- "You asked a question that changed how I saw everything."

- "You didn't tell me what to do. You helped me remember what I already knew."

- "You were thinking with me, not for me."

And that's the core of both coaching and thought partnership—showing up with presence, curiosity, and a fierce belief in someone else's potential.

You've walked with me through this book—from early signs of influence, through powerful practices, to the possibility of coaching as a profession. And, perhaps even more importantly, you've seen how this way of being can evolve into something greater:

- A leadership lens

- A cultural influence

- A thought leadership identity

- A legacy that shapes how others lead

So no matter where you go from here—whether you pursue credentials, deepen your coaching craft, or continue to lead with insight and care—know this:

You are already doing the work. And the world needs more of it.

You should be a coach, and you already are!

A Message from Daphne

I'M DAPHNE B. LATIMORE, SPHR, HCS, CEC—a human capital strategist, executive thought partner, and author of *You Should Be a Coach*, part of my leadership trilogy alongside *Human Capital at the Core* and *The Power of Presence.*

For over 30 years, I've worked alongside leaders, teams, and organizations to navigate complexity with clarity, align culture with strategy, and bring humanity back into the workplace. I'm the Managing Partner of DB Latimore Professional Services Group, a boutique consultancy specializing in HR infrastructure, leadership development, and culture transformation.

My approach blends data-driven insight with coaching presence and behavioral science. I hold certifications in Strategic HR (SPHR), Human Capital Strategy (HCS), and Executive Coaching (CEC), and I bring deep experience across the corporate, nonprofit, and public sectors.

This book was born out of the quiet moments I've witnessed in coaching rooms, breakrooms, and boardrooms—the moments when someone says, "That helped," or "You should be a coach."

Not because of credentials, but because of how they felt after being heard.

My work is rooted in helping leaders show up with clarity, curiosity, and intention—whether they wear the title of coach or not. Because real coaching isn't confined to a profession. It's a way of thinking, leading, and holding space for others to grow.

If this book resonated with you—if you've ever been the person others turn to for perspective, support, or just a better question—I'd love to continue the conversation.

Let's explore how we can:

- Equip your leaders with real-world coaching skills

- Train teams to influence behavior, not just manage performance

- Build a coaching culture rooted in presence, partnership, and practice

- Develop internal capacity through coaching-based leadership development

You can reach out to me via my website:

https://www.dblatimore.com

Or connect with me on LinkedIn:

https://www.linkedin.com/in/daphneblatimore

Because, more than ever—you should be a coach.

Appendix

Coaching vs. Thought Partnership

This chart illustrates the distinction between coaching and thought partnership, highlighting how each approach shapes the conversation, the flow of ideas, and the path to action.

Coaching	Thought Partnership
Focuses on asking powerful questions to guide self-discovery	Engages in mutual problem-solving and idea generation
Facilitates reflection without offering direct solutions	Offers perspective and shares expertise alongside inquiry
Follows a structured process or framework	Adapts fluidly to emerging needs and directions
Centers the client's agenda entirely	Balances both parties' insights for co-created outcomes
Encourages accountability through follow-up	Encourages action through shared ownership of ideas

Sample Polarity Map: Structure vs. Flexibility

This example illustrates how leaders can manage the tension between structure and flexibility.

Structure (Left Pole)	Flexibility (Right Pole)
Clarity in roles and responsibilities	Adaptability to changing needs
Consistent processes and standards	Innovation and creativity
Predictable outcomes	Responsive problem-solving
Risk: Becoming rigid or bureaucratic	Risk: Becoming chaotic or inconsistent

Greater Fear: Losing the ability to deliver results due to either excessive rigidity or disorganized chaos.

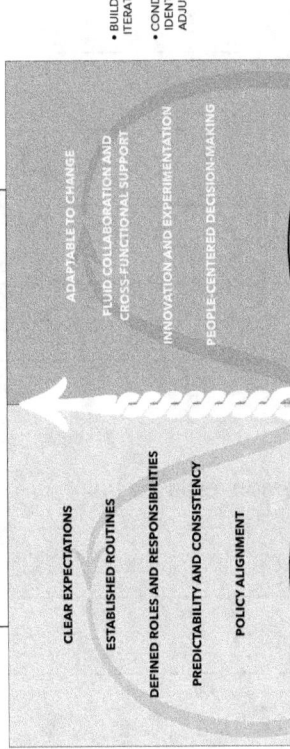

TO LEAD WITH CLARITY WHILE REMAINING ADAPTABLE IN DYNAMIC ENVIRONMENTS.

STRUCTURE AND FLEXIBILITY

STRUCTURE

CLEAR EXPECTATIONS

ESTABLISHED ROUTINES

DEFINED ROLES AND RESPONSIBILITIES

PREDICTABILITY AND CONSISTENCY

POLICY ALIGNMENT

MICROMANAGEMENT

RESISTANCE TO CHANGE

INFLEXIBLE SYSTEMS THAT STIFLE CREATIVITY

FLEXIBILITY

ADAPTABLE TO CHANGE

FLUID COLLABORATION AND CROSS-FUNCTIONAL SUPPORT

INNOVATION AND EXPERIMENTATION

PEOPLE-CENTERED DECISION-MAKING

AMBIGUITY AND CONFUSION

LACK OF ACCOUNTABILITY

CONSTANT SHIFTING OF PRIORITIES

- DEFINE NON-NEGOTIABLES THAT PROVIDE CLARITY AND DIRECTION.
- ESTABLISH COMMUNICATION ROUTINES THAT MAINTAIN STRUCTURE WITHOUT STIFLING AGILITY.

- TEAM DISENGAGEMENT DUE TO RIGIDITY
- DELAYED RESPONSES TO UNEXPECTED CHANGES
- OVERRELIANCE ON PROCEDURES INSTEAD OF JUDGMENT

- BUILD IN TIME FOR EMERGENCY ITERATION, AND EXPERIMENTATION.
- CONDUCT RETROSPECTIVES TO IDENTIFY WHAT'S WORKING AND ADJUST ACCORDINGLY.

- MISSED DEADLINES DUE TO LACK OF PRIORITIZATION
- CONFLICTING INTERPRETATIONS OF DIRECTION
- REPEATED REINVENTION OF PROCESSES

THE GREATEST FEAR OF STRUCTURE IS CHAOS; THE GREATEST FEAR OF FLEXIBILITY IS STAGNATION.

Daily/Weekly Intention Template

Use this template to ground yourself and your coaching practice in clarity and purpose each day or week.

Today, I will focus on

_____

_____

_____

_____

_____

The energy I want to bring into my conversations is

_____

_____

_____

_____

_____

One person I will intentionally support today is

_____

_____

_____

_____

_____

My primary focus for this week is

_____

_____

_____

_____

_____

One habit I will strengthen this week is

_____

_____

_____

_____

_____

I will measure success this week by

_____

_____

_____

_____

_____

Conversation Starters to Use in Real Life

These open-ended questions encourage deeper thinking, reflection, and dialogue in everyday settings:

- What's the most important thing you're working on right now?

- What's one thing that would make this easier for you?

- What's a recent win you're proud of?

- What's getting in the way of your progress?

- If you could wave a magic wand, what would change tomorrow?

- What's a perspective you haven't considered yet?

- What would success look like in six months?

Reviews

"I was fortunate to partner with Daphne while leading a US/UK-based business—me as the British manager and Daphne heading up our U.S. operations. Together, we faced the emotionally difficult task of making redundant colleagues who were also our friends. While U.S. legislation makes the process straightforward, we chose to challenge it, asking why we couldn't treat our U.S. colleagues with the same respect and support their British counterparts received, including outplacement services. We did just that.
Reading You Should Be a Coach brought back many of those moments—times when we were 'coaching' without even calling it that. The book is experiential and authentic, reflecting Daphne's true strengths as a strategic influencer and leader."
—David Ashton
Senior HR Consultant & Director

"Daphne Latimore's You Should Be a Coach is both a guide and a mirror, challenging leaders to see coaching not as a role, but as a mindset rooted in curiosity, humility, and belief in others. With vivid metaphors and practical insights, Latimore distinguishes between coaching—listening and drawing out answers—and thought partnership—collaborating and co-creating ideas. She demonstrates the power of blending the two, enabling leaders to build authentic connections that unlock growth and potential. More than theory,

this book is about impact: a call to lead with presence and purpose. Read it, reflect on it, and live it."
—Jerome L. Haynesworth, CLTMC
Managing Director

"One thing that stood out in You Should Be a Coach was how applicable the content is. Daphne's insights can be put into practice right away. I appreciated how each chapter includes activities, which makes learning hands-on rather than theoretical. The appendix is another gem, with practical templates and conversation starters to return to. Having worked on a team led by Daphne, reading it felt like stepping back to our morning coffee conversations. Many of those helped me reflect on the type of leader I wanted to become. This book is a thought-provoking resource for any development toolkit."
—Ruthmarie Swisher
Leadership & Team Effectiveness Director

"You Should be a Coach is an insightful guide for aspiring coaches, leaders, and those interested in self-coaching. The author blends practical tips with engaging anecdotes, making the coaching journey relatable and inspiring. Each chapter is filled with actionable insights on essential coaching skills and thought partnerships, empowering readers to confidently pursue their passions. This book simplifies the coaching process, making it a quick and enjoyable read for anyone looking to make a meaningful impact on themselves and others.
To my colleague, peer coach, and friend—well done, Daph! You're not at all acting brand new!"
—Karen O. Drake, MA, PCC
Wellness & Executive Coach

www.ingramcontent.com/pod-product-compliance
Lightning Source LLC
Chambersburg PA
CBHW071327130626
46556CB00004B/1782